GW00370548

Stag Nights

Nights

*...and other
great nights
out with the boys!*

Created by
Sonya Winner & Ilana Salem

Thank you to:

Judith and Adam Apter, Colin Bowling, Julia and Philip Burton, Charlie Carmen, John Catto, Charles Cordell, Mike Dawson, Katie Cowan, Lydia Drukarz, Stephen Fisher, Paul Forrester, Andrew Franklin, Ruth and Harold Glickman, Ingrid and Andy Goodman, Tim Jackson, Anna Josse, Neville and Susan Kahn, Jeannette Kupferman, Dee Lahiri, Katie Mierens, Laura Morris, Moss Bros, Tony Mulliken, Mysteries, Simon Olswang, Louise Peters, John Pickard, Natasha Pollard, Claudia and Gina Pollinger, Charles Salem, Claudette and Elliot Salem, Ann Summers, Elizabeth Sutton-Klein, Abner Stein, Daniel Tasker, Ruth Thompson, Lex van Dam, Gozi Wamuo, Barry Winkleman, Daniel Winner and Mary Winner and Paul Winner.

First published in 1999 by André Deutsch Limited
76 Dean Street
London W1V 5HA
http://www.vci.co.uk
André Deutsch is a subsidiary of VCI plc

A catalogue record for this book is available from the British Library
ISBN 0 233 99485 8   Printed in Belgium

Credits:

Created by Sonya Winner and Ilana Salem
Written by Ilana Salem
Design, Art Direction and Co-ordination by Sonya Winner
Hen illustrations by Rachael Busch
Photomontage by Sonya Winner using Adobe Photoshop 5
Gift illustrations by Jacqueline Nicholls
Photography by Colin Bowling and James Johnson
Modelling by Natasha Pollard
Edited by Anna Kiernan and Louise Dixon

To Samuel

for your Stag Night

Dear Chief Stag,

Everyone knows that organizing your best mate's big night out is a heavy responsibility. But do not fear, help is at hand in the form of our essential, definitive guide to Stag Nights.

Let us help you make this a fun, memorable and successful experience. We've covered all types of Stag:

The Jack the Lad Stag

The Shy and Retiring Stag

The Cultured Stag

The New Age Stag *and*

The Outrageously Wild Stag

We've also devised other great nights out for each kind of guy. What's more, there are success and disaster stories told by real live Stags, plus great ideas for Stag presents and the Essential Directory of entertainment, transport, and tailor-made weekends. In fact everything you'll need to make this a night to remember.

Enjoy, and Happy Hunting!

What type of Stag?

What should you do?

Go Hen spotting!	*In the hole!*
Lots of eastern promise	*Sculpture vulture*
Dirty comics	*Anyone for tennis?*
Club fever	*Fishing for a catch*
Doggy Style	*Painting for pleasure*
Farmer Giles	*I am sailing*
Walk on the wild side	*Walk this way*
A spot of birdwatching	*Mad Max*
Get smashed at snooker	*Mile High Club*
Be bowled over	*Paintballing*
Music appreciation, darling	*Bungee Jumping*

The Do's & Don'ts of Stag Nights

Do get drunk but don't get aggressive. It's no fun getting into fights with the local skinheads. After all, no one wants to see a beaten-up groom with three teeth missing on his wedding day.

Do consider the personality of the Stag. If he is a quiet and retiring type he won't appreciate being undressed by two strippers emerging from under the table.

Do take the number of a local mini-cab with you. None of you will be in a fit state to drive and you'll probably need a helping hand to get home.

Don't have the Stag Night the night before the wedding. Stags have been known to be too comatosed to attend their own wedding.

Don't show the lurid photos from the Stag Night to Great Aunt Enid, or any other guests at the wedding for that matter. It's not in good taste.

Don't tell your girlfriend or wife intimate details of the evening. They might be best friends with the future bride-to-be and may not appreciate your sordid goings on.

Don't get personal with the Stag about his new bride. He may not want the world and his wife knowing about the details of his sex life. But talking about exes is fine!

Jack the Lad STAG

He is joined at the hip with 'his mates' who he has to see at least four nights a week. Loves doing really boyish things, like riding motor bikes, go-kart racing and doing up kit cars. Beyond the laddish exterior is his Mum, still doing his washing and ironing every Sunday and cooking his breakfast. Favourite expression is, 'treat 'em mean, keep 'em keen.' Meanwhile, he threatened suicide when his fiancée tried to finish with him over his philandering. Loves wearing brand names and always has his trainers undone à la Noel Gallagher. Met his fiancée at a Legalize Cannabis demo. Pretends to have been forced into marriage by his girlfriend but is secretly looking for a mother replacement.

≈

Likely to get totally drunk at his wedding and become entangled in a rugby scrum with his mates on the dance floor. Bride be warned – he's likely to arrange to meet up with his mates for a pint while on honeymoon.

Organizing *Jack the Lad*
Stag Nights

Go Hen spotting!

Ring round local restaurants to see if any of them have Hen Nights booked the same evening. Try to wangle it so that your party is the only group of Stags amongst a crowd of legless, desperate Hens!

Lots of eastern promise

Have a meal at your local Greek or Turkish restaurant with plenty of plate spinning, dancing on the tables and belly dancing or stripping, depending on if you find the right girl. Top this off with a little gambling at the local casino and try to go home a bit richer.

Dirty comics

Go to a really filthy comedy show with a few X-rated comedians. After a few pints encourage the groom to get on stage and perform his own repertoire.

Club fever

Go to a club and rave like you're seventeen again (unless you are seventeen!). Start a competition based on how many chicks' phone numbers you can collect, or play Bar Cricket, i.e. on your way over to the bar to get a drink try to score as many runs as possible; four runs if you touch one boob or six runs for touching both boobs. No contact, you're out of the game. Make sure you bring pen and paper for accurate scoring!

Doggy Style

Go for dinner at the dogs, have tons of bets and if you collectively win a decent amount, buy your Stag a share in an appropiately named greyhound as a wedding gift.

Shy & Retiring
STAG

He's the type that wears jumbo cords, cardigans and tweed jackets with patches on the arms. He did smoke a pipe for a while, à la Val Doonican, but now only rarely (not politically correct).Works in one of the solitary professions such as gardening, bee keeping, accounting, or as a stand-up comic or writer, but could equally be an extremely successful, but very quiet, high flyer. Friends and neighbours likely to say, 'He's such a lovely boy. He'd do anything for anyone.'

Likely to have met fiancée at a creative writing class, garden centre or walking tour. Loves to have evenings in, cooking and listening to jazz or similar instrumental arrangements. Getting him drunk could result in him reading out past poetry attempts. Honeymoon likely to be a camping holiday in the glorious UK countryside, so forget packing the sexy underwear and stilettos.

Organizing
Shy & Retiring
Stag Nights

Farmer Giles

Experience the reality of country life by cleaning out pig sties, milking cows, lambing from January to March, harvesting in August, ploughing in September, calving in October. Price includes a wholesome lunch and a ride on a tractor, if you ask nicely. Top it all off with plenty of cider during well earnt breaks – oo, argh!

Walk on the wild side

Wildlife weekend courses are run all over England. It's a great opportunity to see badgers, bats, butterflies, flowers and even dolphins and porpoises if you go to the coast. Over 500 short courses offer a wide choice of subjects relating to the countryside and the environment. Very educational and a chance to use binoculars!

A spot of birdwatching

If you don't fancy a strip club then a spot of concentrated birdwatching with amateur and professional ornithologists – could be just the job. Discover falcons, kingfishers, eagles, red kites, woodpeckers and if you're really lucky you may see a few tits.

Get smashed at snooker

A well appointed snooker club opened by Stephen Hendry with excellent bar facilities. Coaching by Pro/Am instructors for individuals or groups of any standard. A great chance to get completely legless.

Be bowled over

There's nothing like lining up your bowls and your pints with a few friends. There are bowling places all over the UK – just split into teams and put your best arm forward! Lots of opportunity for chatting up fellow girlie bowlers.

Cultured STAG

*Wears round glasses like John Lennon and doesn't
wash his hair too often. Went through a phase
of wearing bow ties à la Robin Day in the 80s
but has now grown out of it. Always has his head
in a book. Well educated, well bred and could have
a tendency to be well boring. Works in one of the
professions, maybe as a lawyer, accountant, doctor,
journalist or something in telly.*

*Met fiancée at a book reading. Subsequent dates
covered plays, obscure films with subtitles, theatre,
sculpture and photography exhibitions. Wedding will
be the height of sophistication and very Brideshead
Revisited! Bride-to-be needs plenty of stamina for
the honeymoon, where she's likely to be going to
a European City and visiting four churches, three
cathedrals and two doge's palaces before breakfast.*

14

Organizing

Cultured

Stag Nights

Music appreciation, darling

Strictly for lovers of classical music, you can take a group of highbrow Stags on a music appreciation weekend. Visit the different locations where British composers drew inspiration to write some of their most important works. Weekend breaks are also available for many of Britain's other top music festivals.

In the hole!

The perfect executive sport and a golden opportunity to bond. You can play golf at some of the most scenically beautiful courses in Britain. Check out the best courses in Europe, as voted in *Golf World*. Accommodation ranges from local B & B's to exclusive Georgian manor Houses. Rather lovely.

Sculpture vulture

Arty types will love a weekend sculpture course. All equipment is usually provided and courses are run in a very well equipped studio. Maximum group size is five. Accommodation may be available on the premises, although you can stay at B & B's nearby. Let your creative juices flow during the evening over a few pints of lager at the local pub.

Anyone for tennis?

Brush up your tennis skills with a variety of coaching courses available in the UK. These summer courses are often located at places which boast superb facilities, including a swimming pool, squash courts and sports complex. There is top-class coaching from qualified staff, as well as a chance to do other activities including archery and trampolining.

He is the dead spit of Jesus of Nazareth.
He has wild curly hair, wears tie-dye tops and a
crystal round his neck that he picked up at Glastonbury.
Knows everything there is to know about martial arts
and is a qualified Tai Chi teacher. Enjoys long hikes in
the country, hugging trees and feeling at one with nature.
His job could be anything from being 'Something in the
city' to working for the local housing association.
May also be a primary school teacher.

♋

Likely to have a split identity. His work name
could be Paul whilst his spiritual name could be
Aura, much to the confusion of his family and
friends. Bride-to-be should be aware that he is
likely to suggest going on a Buddhist retreat for
the honeymoon. He's caring and considerate
as long as you don't upset his energy flow.

Organizing

new *age*

Stag Nights

Fishing for a catch

Spend an extremely relaxing and stress free day or weekend fishing with like minded friends. Choose from salmon fishing, brown or rainbow trout fishing in well-stocked natural lakes on a beautiful country estate. You can also try coarse fishing, where you might catch chub, dace, roach or pike. An instructor is available and tackle is provided. Suitable all year round with plenty of places to stay nearby.

Painting for pleasure

Let your creativity run wild on a one or two day painting course in either watercolour, oil, pastel or still life drawing. If you can't be bothered to do a formal course and feel like being a bit sexy then hire a nude model, get her round to your place and have your Stags sitting on cushions with easels at the ready whilst trying hard to get your perspectives right!

I am sailing

Throw caution to the wind and embark on a short sailing course. Participants can, if they wish, take part in all aspects of sailing and running the vessel; from learning to cook to steering at night. An intense and exhilarating experience. Check that equipment is provided. Lunches or dinner are usually extra.

Walk this way

The ultimate pursuit for New Age Stags who want to feel at one with nature and the great outdoors. There are some spectacular places to walk throughout Britain with amazing views. You can even take walking breaks centred on historical, geological, archaeological, literary or national trail themes. Check out the walking boot and outdoor clothing situation before you go.

Outrageously Wild STAG

*Likes fast cars, fast women and life in the fast lane,
especially when travelling at 140 mph on his Kawasaki
motorbike. Wears designer clothes and spends
a ridiculous amount of time in the shower.
This stag makes Mick Jagger look shy and retiring.
He'll do anything for a 'laff' and loves getting up
to all kinds of pranks.*

✌

*He'll 'try anything once'; sky diving, bungee jumping,
climbing Ben Nevis. It will be very difficult to think of
something novel to do on his Stag Night. Loves to chat
up women and in the past had notches above his bed for
every woman he's wooed. Bride-to-be loves him for
what he is and is used to the guilt presents and excuses.
Will probably pull off some amazing stunt at the
wedding like rollerblading up the aisle. Unofficial photo
album likely to include plenty of moony pics.*

Organizing *Outrageously Wild* Stag Nights

Mad Max

If you're mad about speed then you can choose from a range of whole day or 1 hour courses covering motor racing, car rallying, 4 x 4 off road driving, quad bikes, rally karts, go-karts and test your mental and physical stamina to the end. Nicky Lauder eat your heart out.

Mile High Club

Why not throw caution to the wind and try your hand at hand-gliding and paragliding. Day courses and gift vouchers are available for both beginners and advanced levels. All flying equipment is provided, plus there's a great social scene, with local pubs, restaurants and nightclubs on sight at some places. Make sure fellow Stags don't suffer from vertigo.

The pleasures and pains of Paintballing

It's a perfect excuse to run around the woods playing soldiers and shooting people. On arrival each player is issued with a pouch containing three blue tubes full of paint balls, masks and goggles. It's a great laff and a great way to prove how macho you are, particularly if any fellow Hens are playing. Impress a Hen enough and you may even be lucky enough to get a quick snog behind the bushes!

Bungee Jumping

If jumping down 100m is what turns you on then Bungee Jumping could be the kind of adrenalin rush you need. Do remember that only 10% of people doing their first bungee jump decide to repeat the experience. Make sure you have your beers and curry afterwards!

Real life Stag DISASTER stories

Everyone wants their Stag Night to be a success but unfortunately it doesn't always go smoothly. Here are some examples from real live Stags on how it can all go horribly wrong!

I went on a sailing weekend that was like a 'Carry On' film. The best man had this brainwave that 15 of us would have a jolly time racing 12 boats from Southampton to the Isle of Wight.

We arrived in T-shirts, jeans and docksiders with no waterproofs whatsoever. A few of us had had the sense to bring sweatshirts. After a few hours of sailing it started to rain really heavily and we all needed foul weather gear including wellies. Of course the best man had all the suitable attire but had just omitted to brief us poor sods on what to wear. The first night on board we stopped off at a local pub on route for the obligatory beers and curry. The minute we got back on, the waves started to get choppy and most of us spent a good few hours puking over the sides. The worst thing was that none of us had been told to bring sleeping bags (except the best man and the groom of course) so we spent the night huddled together, freezing our whatnots off in a filthy spare sail.

The next morning we were up at 5.30 a.m. for a five hour race that began at seven. Imagine the scene – most of us were still pissed, we had had no breakfast, it was raining and we were all dressed completely inappropriately. Three days later we received a letter from the best man saying we had scraped the bottom of the boat and had to pay £50 each.

And the moral of the story is...

If you're going on an activity weekend make sure you know what kind of dress or equipment you will need.

Keith from Windsor writes...

A colleague of mine from work (who's a real loser) came into work one day with an announcement that he was marrying this desperate divorcee in a quick 'rush-job' wedding.

Apparently her divorce had just come through, so they wanted to get the wedding over with quickly having waited so long for all the legalities. He told me on the Monday that his Stag do was going to be on the Friday night of the same week, so I immediately got the vibe that it was going to be a disaster. Friday came and I showed up knackered after a week's work at this small pub in some village in the middle of nowhere. The other 'Stags' (ha, ha) that were invited were his dad, uncle, cousin and two sullen looking mates. Everyone except me had driven to the pub so I knew that no-one was exactly going to be letting their hair down.

My colleague sits there over a beer telling us all how his wife-to-be had been abused by her ex-husband and starts going into the most appalling detail. I swear we were almost slitting our wrists by the end of it.

It's Friday night in this tiny country village pub, there were no women in the pub and not a strippagram in sight. When the conversation changed to discussions about DIY and what lawn mowers are the best on the market, I knew it was time to leave. Needless to say I decided to turn down the evening of board games that was being planned at his uncle's house.

And the moral of the story is...
It's usually best to go to a Stag Night where you know the Stag or at least his friends well, otherwise you could be in for a night of boredom!

Callum from Northern Ireland writes...

I was working in Hong Kong as a steel trader in the Eighties and was told one day by my boss that one of our very important Chinese clients was going to be getting married and he wanted me to organize his Stag Night. It was to be a totally lavish, no expenses spared affair, and the brief from my boss was to give him the full red carpet treatment.

Without delay I booked a private room a five star delux hotel and between myself and the head waiter chose a menu with the finest vintage wines and champagnes. I also asked him to recommend some kind of girlie entertainment.

Within an hour he had booked a beautiful, young Thai girl who would perform all kinds of tricks for the guests. The evening had a fantastic start. I had organized drinks on the terrace overlooking the harbour. By the time we had moved on to the brandy everyone was pretty drunk, and getting very excited to see 'Genie the Thai girl'.

At one o'clock this beautiful girl appeared, dressed for action, titillating and teasing everyone. She then got our very important client and removed every item of clothing from him before simulating sex on the dining room table. After 30 minutes of sordid goings on she announced in an extremely low voice 'and the biggest surprise of the evening is the real ME!' before removing her wig revealing Genie was in fact a bloke! Everybody was completely stunned, including our client who threw his clothes on in a fury before storming out.

I got a bollocking from my boss – we did in fact lose the client.

And the moral of the story is...
If you're organizing a 'corporate style' Stag Night
make sure you organize everything yourself.

Real life
Stag
Success

stories Some Stag Nights just have everything
going for them. Usually it's because
there's a wild herd of mates who just
want to have fun without locking antlers!

We started out at the local pub getting well tanked-up and out of our heads. After that we bussed it down to this place called, 'School Boy Fun' which was dead naughty and right up my street. These two women, one blonde, one brunette, met us at the entrance wearing tiny gymslips and school ties with their hair tied up in pigtails. Then this really buxom Headmistress came in waving a cane. She looked just like Hattie Jacques and made us all sit on these really low chairs against a table. She then whipped out a piece of paper from her pocket and in a really loud voice said 'Where is that very naughty little boy Philip Abbot. I want to see how good his multiplication and spelling is.' Everytime I got an answer wrong I got a slipper on my bare, white hairy arse. We did everything from standing in the corner with our pants down to playing pass the schoolgirl!

After hours of humiliation and fun we ended up eating a real school dinner complete with jelly and ice-cream which we each smeared all over the schoolgirls' naughty bits! Before we left, everyone got a punishment of their choice, which I'll leave to your imagination.

And the moral of the story is...
Make sure you do something that the Stag
will really find fun, not embarrassing.

There isn't a bloke in the world who doesn't dream about being a rock 'n' roll star and my brother Nick is no exception.

Because I had contacts in the music biz it was pretty easy and cheap for us to hire a recording studio with the intention of making a record. Five of us piled into the studio armed with a couple of crates of lager, a million packets of fags and it was down to business.

We spent the first few hours playing our favourite records of all time and trying to get inspiration on what kind of music we wanted to make. At first we sounded like Pinky and Perky on drugs, but then one of the guys hit the keyboards, whilst another got out his percussion bits and we had something like a tune going. After hours of bantering we even had a groovy sounding title and name for the band: 'The Sad Stags!'. We had excellent fun messing about with all the machinery too.

It was now 2a.m. and our creative juices were well and truly flowing. After 12 hours of jamming, sampling and arguing in the studio we ended up with a kind of Genesis meets Radiohead, with something that sounded remarkably like Quo thrown in. It was the most brilliant night and it was great to have a record to keep as a souvenir afterwards.

And the moral of the story is...
Fulfilling a real ambition or a fantasy is
a great thing to do on your Stag Night.

I had a really difficult job organizing a Stag Night for eight very different types of men, but in the end it worked absolutely brilliantly.

Since most blokes seem to like a challenge, a day at the Motorcross seemed a great idea. Each session lasts a minimum of 2 hours.

First we got dressed in knee and shin guards, a combined breast and back plate with reinforced pads that flap over the shoulders. Gloves, crash helmet, mouthguard and goggles add the finishing touches, then you're off.

We used small Kawasaki 80cc bikes and basically learnt how to master the circuit, bumps and all. It was exhausting, as you can't just sit down and let the bike do all the work, your body is constantly shifting up and down. The idea is to maintain a constant speed, changing down gears before hitting a corner. It was quite a nerve racking, but very exhilarating, experience.

You use up a lot of calories on Motorcross and afterwards we were incredibly thirsty from inhaling tons of sand and dust. We hit the pub and had lots to talk about. Everyone agreed it was a brilliant day.

And the moral of the story is...
If you try something new it always turns
out to be a great experience and a challenge, too.

heavenly
Stag presents

Here are some tame prezzie suggestions to treat your Stag to, and give him a real good send off before the big day.

Galloping Gourmets
Collectable wines, ports or brandys, gourmet hampers, cookery books, subscription to chocolate society, smelly cheeses.

High Fidelity
CD, CD carrier, cassette, Walkman, Discman, concert tickets. Make a request on the radio and tape it or make up a cassette of your Stag's most raunchy tunes and introduce each track.

Classic Memories
Silver photoframe with picture of Stag's mates mounted inside it. Or make up your own photo montage of the Stag Night or Wedding and put it in an album.

Glam Man
Scarf, leather gloves, silk tie, boxer shorts, waistcoat or socks with a unique design.

Hippy Man
Hammock, candle holder, bong pipe, scented candle, wind chime, set of crystals, joss sticks, bach flower remedies for wedding nerves or hangovers.

Mr Hobby
Old records or manuals of Stag's favourite pop group, back issues of cult comics, anything he collects.

DIY Expert
Tool set, drill, DIY manual, set of paint brushes, screwdrivers, hammer, gift voucher for local DIY store.

Literary Type
Glam coffee table book, love poems, erotic prose, jokey book, loo book or subscription to Stag's favourite mag!

Personal

*Engraved cufflinks,
personlized stationery,
diary, keyring, wallet,
cigar cutter, cigarette
holder, lighter.*

Muscle Man

*Sports bag, sports kit,
weights, football kit
of favourite team.*

Arty Man

*Book featuring Stag's
favourite artist, set of
watercolour or oil
paints, brushes,
canvas, easel, stencil
or caligraphy set,
italic pens, painting
smock.*

**Gentleman's Best
Friends**

*Hipflask, shoe cleaning
kit, manicure or pedicure
set, scissors for extracting
nose or ear hairs.*

Hellish
Hen Presents

Here are some really wicked prezzie suggestions to treat your Stag to. Start the groom blushing before he's even started his wedding day!

The Stud
PVC skimpy briefs complete with matching vest, and full PVC body suit.

Cock-Tail Presents!
Curvaceous straws, Pamela Anderson booby ice cube holders, nude female bottle opener.

Tame Her!
Be-the-boss mask, leather whip, dog collar, plastic handcuffs, schoolgirl cane.

Titivating T-shirts for Him
T-shirts with your own made up OTT statement, e.g. 'I'm legless on Ian's Stag Night'. With the date and location printed on it.

I GOT PISSED AT MARK'S STAG NIGHT!

Off the Wall
Dreamy calendar of your sexiest, fantasy women to drool all over. Design your own 'Countdown to the wedding calendar, with personal messages to your Stag!

Mr Bookworm
Kama Sutra. How to Make Love to the Same Person for the Rest of you Life. 203 Ways to Drive Her to Orgasm. Sex Maniacs Cook Book. Sexy Cocktail Book. 227 Ways to Unleash the Sex Goddess in Every Woman. Men are from Mars, Women are from Venus.

Fantasy Babe
Buy him something he might not be brave enough to get his bride, e.g. a peephole bra, crotchless knickers, nurse's, maid's or French mistress's outfit.

Work that Body
Temporary tattoos, chocolate body paint, wild fruit body paint. Delay spray to keep his member under control.

Bodily Pleasures
Smelly creams to increase sensitivity and intensify orgasm. Lickable and scented massage lotion. 100% natural herbal potion containing aphrodiziacs, or design your own erotic blend of oils from your chemist and label it something apt.

Hello Dolly!

Blonde or brunette blow-up dolls with real hair. A wonderful companion when your partner's out shopping with her mother – just don't get caught in a hot embrace!

X-citing and X-rated

Your fantasy come true with a selection of naughty videos. Alternatively get him a subscription to his favourite dirty mag.

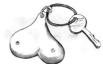

Naughty Exec Fun

Dirty doodle pad, boob keyring, stress buster to squeeze very hard when you're frustrated.

Private Members

A huge variety of creams to keep your member in tip-top condition, like stud action spray, stud delay spray, keep up the erection lotion, KY jelly.

Good Vibrations!

Vibrators for you or her with lots of different names and functions. Choose from big black ones, flesh coloured ones, silver and gold ones, knobbly ones or even ones that look like corn on the cob!

HOLLYWOOD
quotes

In Tinsel Town marriage is still very much
the done thing. The problem is how many
times they do it! Here's what the stars
say about love and the Big M!

'Behind every successful man, you'll find a woman
who has nothing to wear.'
James Stewart

'If you can't stand the heat in the kitchen, stand
nearer the refrigerator'
Bill Cosby

'I always thought music was more important than sex
– then I thought if I don't hear a concert for
a year-and-a-half, it doesn't bother me.'
Jackie Mason

'Staying married may have long-term benefits. You
can elicit much more sympathy from friends over a
bad marriage than you ever can from a good divorce.'
P.J. O'Rourke

'Marriage is a wonderful invention; but then again,
so is a bicycle repair kit.'
Billy Connolly

'Love and marriage, love and marriage
Go together like a horse and carriage.'
Sammy Cahn

'Home is heaven and orgies are vile,
But you need an orgy, once in a while.'
Ogden Nash

Glossary

Here are some classic cockney phrases to thrill your Stag with on the night, or for use in the Best Man's wedding speech. Either way, you'll find they'll give you a real Cow and Calf – Laugh!

China Plate	Mate
Eartha Kitts	Shits
Elephant's Trunk	Drunk
Exchange and Mart	Tart
Fine and Dandy	Brandy
Fog and Mist	Pissed
First Aid Kits	Tits
Fun and Frolics	Bollocks
Kiss of life	Wife
Knotty Ash	Cash
Order the Eighteen Carat	Claret
Never Fear	Beer
Joy Stick	Prick
Oedipus Rex	Sex
Pot and Pan	Man
Rise and Shine	Wine

Here it is... The definitive guide to every Stag activity. We've also included companies specializing in taylor-made Stag Weekends, as well as details of where to get your Stag present.

There are also some great websites worth visiting, for all you surfing Stags out there. A great starting point for your web searches is at www.leisurehunt.com/, where you will find a wealth of information on accommodation, culture, eating and drinking, nature, sport, and travel throughout the UK and abroad.

Activities

Abseiling:
British Mountaineering Council
177/179 Burton Road,
Manchester M20 2BB
Tel: 0161 445 4747
Fax: 0161 445 4500

Adventure Courses:
If you're looking for a 1-5 day multi-activity break then the following suggestions are ideal. They cover a huge variety of activities like archery, abseiling, caving, pot holing, mountain biking, canoeing, orienteering and white water rafting.

Acorn Activities
PO Box 120, Hereford HR4 8YB
Tel: 01432 830083
Fax: 01432 830110
www.acornactivities.co.uk

Anglian Activity
29 Yarmouth Road,
Norwich NR7 OED
Tel: 01603 700 770
Fax: 01603 701 166
www.anglianactivities.co.uk

The Adventure Company
Low Grove Farm,
Millbeck,
Keswick,
Cumbria CA12 4PS
Tel: 017687 75351
Fax: 017687 75763
E-mail:sales@theadventureco.com
www.theadventureco.com

Black Mountain Activities
PO Box 5,
Hay-on-Wye
Herefordshire HR3 5YB
Tel/Fax: 01497 847 897
E-mail:enquires@blackmountain.co.uk
www.blackmountain.co.uk

Edale YHA Activity Centre
Rowland Cote, Nether Booth,
Edale, Hope Valley S33 7ZH
Tel: 014336 70302
www.yha-englandwales.org.uk

**Great Glen School
of Adventure**
Great Glen Water Park,
South Laggan, Spean Bridge,
Inverness-shire PH34 4EA
Tel: 01809 501 381
Fax: 01809 501 218

HF Holidays Ltd
Imperial House, Edgware Road,
London NW9 5AL
Tel: 0181 905 9557
Fax: 0181 205 0506
E-mail:101523.1274@compu
serve.com

Outdoor Adventure
Atlantic Court,Widemouth Bay,
Bude, Cornwall EX23 0DF
Tel: 01288 361 312
Fax: 01288 361 153
E-mail:info@outdooradventure.co.uk
www.outdooradventure.co.uk

Outward Bound
Watermillock, Penrith,
Cumbria CA11 0JL
Tel: 0990 134227
Fax: 017684 86983
www.outwardbound-uk.org

Airsports

**The British Hang-Gliding and
Paragliding Association**
The Old Schoolroom,
Loughborough Road,
Leicester LE4 5PJ
Tel: 01162 611 322
Fax: 01162 611 323
www.bhpa.co.uk

Archery

**Grand National
Archery Society**
Seventh Street,
National Agricultural Centre,
Stoneleigh, Kenilworth
Warwickshire CV8 2LG
Tel: 01203 696 631
Fax: 01203 419 662
www.gnas.u-net.com

Assault Courses

The Outdoor Trust
Windy Gyle,
30 West Street, Belford,
Northumberland NE70 7QE
Tel/Fax: 01668 213 289
E-mail:trust@outdoor.demon.co.uk

Ballooning

Virgin Balloon Flights
Unit 1, Stafford Park 12,
Telford, Shropshire,TF3 3BJ
Tel: 01952 200141
Fax: 01952 290338

E-mail:james.ball@virgin.co.uk
www.virginballoonflights.com

Field Studies Council
Preston Montford,
Montford Bridge, Shrewsbury,
Shropshire SY4 1HW
Tel: 01743 850 674
Fax: 01743 850 178
E-mail: fsc.headoffice@ukonline.co.uk

English Bowling Association
Lyndhurst Road,
Worthing BN11 2AZ
Tel: 01903 820 222
Fax: 01903 820 444

**British Elastic Rope Sports
Association**
33a Canal Street,
Oxford OX2 6BQ
Tel: 01865 311 179
Fax: 01865 311 189

Acorn Activities
(see previous listing under
Adventure Courses)

**Camping and Caravanning UK
Directory** is the internet
resource for camping and
caravanning sites in the UK:
www.camping.uk-directory.com/

British Canoe Union
Adbolton Lane,
West Bridgford,
Nottingham NG2 5AS
Tel: 0115 982 1100

For a comprehensive listing
detailing venues that specialize
in serious motor sports, ask
for the *Starting in Motorsports*
book priced at £3.00 from:

**The RAC Motor Sports
Association Ltd**
Motor Sports House,
Riverside Park,
Colnbrook, Slough
Berkshire SL3 0HG
Tel: 01753 681 736
Fax: 01753 682 938

Brands Hatch Leisure Group
Fawkham, Longfield,
Kent DA3 8NG
Tel: 0990 125 250

**Windsport International
Action Centres**
Central Information,
Mylor Yacht Harbour,

Falmouth, Cornwall TR11 5UF
Tel: 01326 376 191
Fax: 01326 376 192
E-mail:windsport.international
@btinternet.com
www.windsport-int.com

Caving
National Caving Association
C/O Monomark House,
27 Old Gloucester Street,
London WC1N 3XX
(written enquiries only)

Clay Pigeon Shooting
Dedes Hotel &
South West Shooting School
1-4 The Promenade, Ilfracombe,
Devon EX34 9BD
Tel: 01271 862 545
Fax: 01271 862 234

The Merton Hotel
28 Commercial Road,
Hereford HR1 2BD
Tel: 01432 265 925
Fax: 01432 354 983

Newland Hall also specialize
in Stag & Hen Days with
a whole range of activities:
Newland Hall
Roxwell, Chelmsford,
Essex CM1 4LH
Tel: 01245 231 010
Fax: 01245 231 463

Climbing
An informative web site
covering all aspects of climbing
is **Climbing UK**
www.eclimb.com/ukclimb/
**Acorn Activities, Black Mountain
Activities.** (See previous listing
under Adventure Courses) and
British Mountaineering Council
(See previous listing under
Abseiling)

Comedy Clubs
The Comedy Store
1a Oxenden Street
London W1
Tel: 01426 914 433

Jongleurs: Central bookings
Tel: 0171 564 2500
Venues in: Battersea, Camden,
Bow, Leicester, Oxford, Watford,
Southampton and Nottingham

Cookery Weekends
Acorn Activities (see previous
listing under Adventure Courses).
Acorn run two day courses
where you'll learn a selection
of vegetarian, meat and fish
dishes. You can also go on
a cider and wine-tasting
weekend with visits to vineyards,
plus full dinner and wine tasting
on Saturday nights.

Cycling and Mountain Biking

Cyclists Touring Club
Cotterell House,
69 Meadrow, Godalming,
Surrey GU7 3HS
Tel: 01483 417 217
Fax: 01483 426 994
E-mail:cycling@ctc.org.uk

Dinghy Sailing

The Royal Yachting Association is
the national authority
for dinghy and yacht sailing,
motor cruising, windsurfing
and powerboat racing.
Royal Yachting Association
RYA House, Romsey Road,
Eastleigh, Hampshire SO50 9YA
Tel: 01703 627 400
Fax: 01703 629 924
E-mail:admin@rya.org.uk

Diving

British Sub Aqua Club
Telfords Quay, Ellesmere Port,
South Wirral, Cheshire L65 4FY
Tel: 0151 350 6200
Fax: 0151 350 6215
E-mail: bsac@.com

Drawing

Field Studies Council
Preston Montford,
Montford Bridge, Shrewsbury
Shropshire SY4 1HW

Tel: 01743 850 674
Fax: 01743 850 178

Acorn Activites and **HF
Holidays** (See previous listing
under Adventure Courses)

Dry Slope Skiing

English Ski Council
Queensway Mall,
The Cornbow,
Halesowen B63 4AJ
Tel: 0121 501 2314
Fax: 0121 585 6448

Calshot Activities Centre
Calshot Spit,
Fawley, Southampton,
Hampshire SO4 1BR
Tel: 01703 892077
Fax: 01703 891267

Farming

(See National Tourist Board's
Stay on a Farm book published
by Jarrold.)

Fishing

Acorn Activities (See previous
listing under Adventure
Courses)

Flower arranging

One day courses in practical
floristry, fresh and dry flowers
and tuition arranging bouquets,
posies and sprays.

Acorn Activities (See previous listing under Adventure Courses)

Flying
The British Microlight Aircraft Association
Head Office BMAA
Bullring,
Deddington,
Banbury,
Oxon OX15 OTT
Tel: 01869 338888
Fax: 01869 337116
E-mail: bma@avnet.co.uk
www.avnet.co.uk/bmaa/bmaa.htm

Gambling
For a list of over 20 casinos:
Stakis Regency Casinos
Tel: 0171 833 1881

Gardening
One day courses available at
Acorn Activities (See previous listing under Adventure Courses)

Go Karting
Playscape has tracks in Battersea and Streatham:
Playscape
Battersea Karts Raceway
Hester Road,
London SW11 4AN
Tel: 0171 801 0110
Fax: 0171 801 0111
www.playscape.co.uk

Gliding
British Gliding Association
Kimberly House,
Vaughan Way,
Leicester, LE1 4SE
Tel: 0116 253 1051
Fax: 0116 251 5939
E-mail: Bgahq@aol.com

Golf
For a wealth of information on everything related to golf, try these two web sites:
www.leisurehunt.com/
www.golfweb.co.uk

Greyhound Racing
Wimbledon Stadium
Tel: 0181 946 8000

Catford Stadium
Tel: 0181 690 8000

Wembley Stadium
Tel: 0181 902 8833 ext: 3412

Helicopter Flights
British Helicopter Advisory Board
Graham Suite,
Fairoaks Airport,
Chobham, Woking,
Surrey GU24 8HX
Tel: 01276   856 100
Fax: 01276   856 126
www.bhab.demon.co.uk

Holistic/Complete Indulgence

Foxhills Country Club arrange *Complete Indulgence Days* at the Foxgloves Health Spa. Residents of Foxhills Country Club have free access to tennis, 3 swimming pools, a 9 hole golf course and gym. There are 3 restaurants and 4 private dining rooms:
Foxhills Country Club
Stone Hill Road,
Ottershaw, Surrey KT16 0EL
Tel: 01932 872 050
Fax: 01932 875 200

Oakley Court Hotel is a splendid Gothic hotel with beautiful gardens, spa *(with a full compliment of beauty treatments)* plus leisure club including golf and tennis. Boat trips on the Thames available. There is a restaurant and private dining rooms:
Oakley Court Hotel
Windsor Road, Water Oakley,
Windsor, SL4 5UR
Tel: 01753 609 988
Fax: 01628 637011
E-mail: oakleyct@atlas.co.uk

The Sanctuary
A great health spa in the heart of Covent Garden.

11-12 Floral Street
London WC2E 9DH
Tel: 0171 420 5151
Fax:0171 497 0410

Wolfcastle Pottery offer creative pottery, coastal walks and aromatherapy for up to 12 people at one time at:
Wolfcastle Pottery
Pembrokeshire SA62 5LZ
Tel/Fax: 01437 741 609
www.pbiorg.uk

Horse Racing
The Jockey Club
42 Portman Square,
London W1H 0EN
Tel: 0171 486 4921
E-mail:info@thejockeyclub.co.uk
www.thejockeyclub.co.uk

Horse Riding
The British Horse Society
Stoneleigh, Kenilworth,
Warwickshire CV8 2ZR
Tel: 01926 707 700
Fax: 01926 707 800
E-mail:enquiry@bhs.org.uk

Jet Skiing
Jet Ski UK also do Go Karting and Quad Biking.
Jet Ski UK
Lake 11, Spine Road,
Cotswold, Water Park,

Cirencester, Glos GL7 6DF
Tel: 01285 861 345
Fax: 01285 861 828

Microlighting
The British Microlight Aircraft Association
Head Office, Bullring,
Deddington, Banbury,
Oxon OX15 0TT
Tel: 01869 338 888
Fax: 01869 337 116

Motorcross
Auto Cycle Union
Wood Street, Rugby,
Warkickshire CV21 2YX
Tel: 01788 540 519
Fax: 01788 573 585
E-mail:admin@acu.org.uk
www.acu.org.uk

Mountain Biking
Cyclists Touring Club
Cotterell House
69 Meadrow, Godalming
Surrey GU7 3HS
Tel/Fax: 01483 417217
E-mail: Cycling@ctc.org.uk
www.ctc.org.uk

Murder Mystery Weekends
Use your detective skills and try to solve the plot to reveal the murderer. Actors pose as guests, clues are dropped, the plot unfolds and it's up to you to say whodunnit.

Acorn Activities and **HF Holiday Ltd** (See previous listing under Adventure Courses)

National Trust Regional Offices
Northern Ireland
Tel: 01238 510 721
Fax: 01238 511 242
Wales
Tel: 01558 822 800
Fax: 01558 822 872
South England
Tel: 01372 453 401
Fax: 01372 452 023
North West England
Tel: 01539 435 599
Fax: 01539 435 353

Off Road Driving
The Federation of Off-road Driving Schools
Mandie Chester Bristow
PO Box 9, Hoyland, Barnsley,
South Yorks S74 0YY
Tel: 01226 748 822
Fax: 01226 740 151
E-mail: spectrum.cp@ao1.com

Paintball
The United Kingdom Paintballing Sports Federation
41 Cedar Road, Hutton,
Brentwood,Essex CM13 1NS

Parachuting

British Parachuting Association
5 Wharfway, Glen Parva,
Leicester LE2 9TF
Tel: 0116 278 5271
Fax: 0116 247 7662
E-mail:skydive@bpa.org.uk
www.bpa.org.uk

Wild Geese Sky-Diving Centre
116 Carrowreagh Road,
Garvagh, Coleraine,
Co. Londonderry BT51 5LQ
Tel: 01266 558 609
Fax: 01266 557 050

Paragliding

The British Hang-Gliding and Paragliding Association
The Old School Room,
Loughborough Road,
Leicester LE4 5PJ
Tel: 0116 261 1322
Fax: 0116 261 1323
E-mail: office@bhpa.co.uk
www.bhpa.co.uk

Performing Arts

For a comprehensive listings service of opera, concerts, theatre and ballet venues and events and gift ideas, go to the following sites:
www.whatsonstage.com/
www.lifestyle.co.uk/

Polo Clubs

For general enquires about polo:
www.polonet.co.uk

Scotland
Edinburgh Polo Club
Tel: 0131 449 6696
Fax: 0131 333 1331

England
Ascot Park Polo Club
Tel: 0134 462 1312

Potholing

National Caving Association
Monomark House,
27 Old Gloucester St,
London WC1N 3XX
E-mail: nca@ukonline.co.uk

Pottery

Acorn Activities (see previous listing under Adventure Courses)

Psychic

You can organize a host of psychic experiences including seances, tarot readings, crystal ball, astrology, palm readings at: **Mysteries** – London's Psychic Shop and New Age Centre:
Mysteries
9-11 Monmouth Street,
London WC2H 9DA
Tel: 0171 240 3688
Fax: 0171 240 4845

E-mail:events@mysteries.co.uk
www.mysteries.co.uk

To find your local club contact:
Lawn Tennis Association
The Queen's Club
Barons Court, West Kensington,
London W14 9EG
Tel: 0171 381 7000
Fax: 0171 381 3773

Current Trends
Adbolton Lane,West Bridgford,
Nottingham NG2 5AS
Tel: 01159 818 844
Fax: 01159 822 033

The Scottish Rafting Association
Traditional rafting plus the
latest sensation *Canadian
Canoeing* (Old Red Indian Style
canoes for up to 9 passengers !)
Scottish Voyageurs
Upper Wharf, Canal Side,
Fort Augustus,
Inverness-shire PH32 4AV
Tel: 01320 366 666
Fax: 01320 366 636

The Welsh Rafting Committee
Pioneer Activities
Waen Fawr, Pentrecelyn,
Ruthin, Denbighshire LL15 2HW
Tel/Fax: 01978 790 485
E-mail:pioneer.activities@virgin.net

Ramblers' Association
1-5 Wandsworth Road,
London SW8 2XX
Tel: 0171 339 8500
Fax: 0171 339 8501

Outward Bound organize short
breaks in rock climbing, walking,
scrambling and mountaineering
in a variety of different locations.
Outward Bound, Watermillock,
Penrith, Cumbria CA11 OJL
Tel: 0990 134 227
Fax: 0176 848 6983
E-mail:enquiries@outwardbound-uk.org
www.outwardbound-uk.org

Bowles Outdoor Centre is a
purpose built centre an hour from
London that offers activities
including rock climbing /abseiling,
canoeing, skiing, orienteering, ropes
course, zip wire and problem solving.
Bowles Outdoor Centre
Eride Green,Tunbridge Wells,
Kent TN3 9LW
Tel: 01892 665 665
Fax: 01892 669 556

See Windsport International
Action Centres (see previous
listing under Catamaran Sailing)

Sculpture

Henry Moore's former assistant Peter Hibbard offers expert tuition in his own well equipped studio for weekend courses in clay modelling, rubber mould making, woodcarving and stonecarving.

Old School Arts Workshop
Top Cross, Midleham, Leyburn, North Yorkshire DL8 4QG
Tel: 01969 623 056

Snooker

Acorn Activities (See previous listing under Adventure Courses)

Snowboarding

English Ski Council
Queensway Mall,
The Cornbow,
Halesowen B63 4AJ
Tel: 0121 501 2314
Fax: 0121 585 6448

Surfing

British Surfing Association (BSA)
Champions Yard, Penzance, Cornwall TR18 2TA
Tel: 01736 360 250
Fax: 01736 331 077

Tank Driving

The Activity Superstore
PO Box 123
Saffron, Walden, Essex CB10 1XX

Tel: 01799 526 526
Fax: 01799 526 528
E-mail:superstore@dial.pipex.com
www.serve.co.uk/superstore

Theme Parks

For an index of UK theme parks such as Chessington, Alton Towers and Butlin's, look at: www.leisurehunt.com/

Water Skiing

British Water Ski Federation
390 City Road,
London EC1V 2QA
Tel: 0171 833 2855
Fax: 0171 837 5879
E-mail:info@bwsf.co.uk
www.bwsf.co.uk

Wind Surfing

**Lochore Meadows
Windsurfing School**
Lochore Meadows Country Park, Crosshill, By Lochgelly, Fife KY5 8BA
Tel: 01592 860 264
Fax: 01592 414 345

West Wales Windsurfing and Sailing
Dale, Nr Haverfordwest, Pembrokeshire SA62 3RB
Tel/Fax: 01646 636 642

Rickmansworth Windsurfing and Canoeing Centre
The Aquadrome, Frogmore Lane,
Rickmansworth, Herts WD3 2DH
Tel/Fax: 01923 771 120

Yachting

Windsport International has
sites throughout the UK which
include water-skiing, sailing,
surfing, canoeing, power-
boating, yachting, tube riding,
windsurfing and catamaran
sailing.

Mylor Yacht harbour
Falmouth, Cornwall TR11 5UF
Tel: 01326 376 191
Fax: 01326 376 192
E-mail: windsport.
international@btinternet.com
Web: www.windport-int.com

Yoga

Include a stamped addressed
envelope for information on
retreats and practitioners in
your area to.

British Wheel of Yoga
1 Hamilton Place, Boston Road
Sleaford, Linconshire NG34 7ES
Tel/Fax: 01529   303233
E-mail: wheelyoga@aol.com
http://members.aol.com/wheelyoga

Tailor-made Trips

Trips abroad

The Air Travel Advisory Bureau
gives details of agents selling
competitively priced flights and
on occasion accommodation to
all destinations.
Tel: 0171 636 5000

International Train Enquires
Tel: 0990 848848

Amsterdam

Alternative Amsterdam
A website featuring Stag and Hen
weekends to Amsterdam.
www.bus.co.uk/hotel-uk/amredlt.html

Amsterdam Express
Party coach weekender from
Bournemouth via Southampton
and Portsmouth to Amsterdam.
Amsterdam Express
203 Victory Business Centre,
Portsmouth, Hants PO1 1PJ
Tel: 0705 782222
E-mail:amstr@worldservice. powernet-int.co.uk

Club Med
106 Brompton Road,
London SW3 1JJ
Tel: 0171 581 1161
Fax: 0171 589 6086
www.clubmed.com

Eurostar

Plan a surprise ski trip for the groom-to-be, or regress to your childhood by taking the train to Disneyland Paris for a weekend!

Disneyland Paris
Tel: 0990 030303

Eurostar Ticket Office
102-104 Victoria Street,
London SW1 5JL
Tel: 0990 186186

Trips in the UK

National Railway Enquires
Tel: 0345 484950

English Tourist Board
Thames Tower, Blacks Road,
Hammersmith, London W6 9EL
Tel: 0181 846 9000
Fax: 0181 563 0302
www.visitbritain.com

London Tourist Board
6th Floor, Glen House,
Stag Place, London SW1E 5LT
Tel: 0839 123456*
*Calls cost 45p per minute cheap rate,
50p per minute at all other times*

Scottish Tourist Board
23 Ravelston Terrace,
Edinburgh, EH4 3EU
Tel: 0131 332 2433

Fax: 0131 343 1513
www.holiday.scotland.net

Wales Tourist Board
1 Regent's Street,
London SW1Y 4XT
Tel: 0171 808 3838
Fax: 0171 808 3830
www.vistwales.co.uk

Youth Hostel Association
Trevelyan House,
8 St Stephens Hill,
St Albans AL1 2DY
Tel: 01727 845 047
Fax: 01727 844 126
E-mail:yhacustomerservice
@compuserve.com
www.yha.org.uk

Dublin

Dublin is becoming the Hen and Stag weekend destination. Bord Falite, the Irish Tourist Board, cites it as the most popular shortbreak destination in Europe.

Bord Failte   (The Irish Tourist Board)
150 New Bond Street,
London W1Y OAQ
Tel: 0171 493 3201
Fax: 0171 493 9065

Edinburgh

Edinburgh Stag Weekends
600 Pubs, B & B to 5 star